Writers Who Changed the World

I0644464

JANE AUSTEN

Anita Croy

LUCENT
PRESS

Published in 2020 by
Lucent Press, an Imprint of Greenhaven Publishing, LLC
353 3rd Avenue
Suite 255
New York, NY 10010

Produced for Lucent by Calcium
Editors: Sarah Eason and Tim Cooke
Designers: Paul Myerscough and Lynne Lennon
Picture researcher: Rachel Blount

Picture credits: Cover: Shutterstock: Slonomysh; Inside: Shutterstock: BasPhoto: pp. 7t, 18; Chrisdorney: pp. 8, 41b; Mark Dozier: p. 56; Everett – Art: p. 54; Everett Historical: pp. 37, 39, 42, 44; Fenton one: p. 9; Gangoo: p. 11; David Hughes: p. 61t; Kathy Hutchins: p. 61b; Gail Johnson: p. 24; Andy Lidstone: pp. 40, 41t; Dmitry Naumov: p. 17; Vera Petruk: p. 26; PhotoFires: pp. 16, 59; Pxl.store: p. 52; Valdis Skudre: p. 15; Tviolet: p. 58; Adrian Zenz: pp. 22, 60; Wikimedia Commons: p. 51b; James Andrews: p. 4; From a watercolour by James Andrews of Maidenhead based on an unfinished work by Cassandra Austen. Engraving by William Home Lizars: p. 57; George Atkinson & T.C.P. & Charles Joseph Hullmandel: p. 20; Jane Austen: pp. 27t, 27b, 55; William Blake: p. 51t; C.E. Brock: p. 28; Branwell Brontë: p. 46; Sir Frederick Burton: p. 47; Steve F-E-Cameron: p. 48; Jacques-Louis David: p. 21t; James B. Dennis: p. 21r; Harris Brisbane Dick Fund, 1917: p. 50; John Hoppner: p. 36; Thomas Lawrence: p. 12; J. McNeven: p. 14; William Henry Mote: p. 19; Alfred Pearse: p. 45; Giuseppe Piattoli: p. 35; Pickering & Greatbatch: p. 31; William Bell Scott: p. 32; The British Library: p. 25; Elizabeth Thompson: p. 38; Hugh Thomson: pp. 29, 30; Theodore Von Holst: p. 49.

Cataloging-in-Publication Data

Names: Croy, Anita.
Title: Jane Austen / Anita Croy.
Description: New York : Lucent Press, 2020. | Series: Writers who changed the world | Includes glossary and index.
Identifiers: ISBN 9781534565845 (pbk.) | ISBN 9781534565852 (library bound) | ISBN 9781534565869 (ebook)
Subjects: LCSH: Austen, Jane, 1775-1817--Juvenile literature. | Novelists, English--19th century--Biography--Juvenile literature.
Classification: LCC PR4036.C79 2020 | DDC 823'.7 B--dc23

Printed in the United States of America

CPSIA compliance information: Batch #BS19KL: For further information contact Greenhaven Publishing LLC, New York, New York at 1-844-317-7404.

CONTENTS

CHAPTER 1

This is a portrait of Jane Austen.

JANE AUSTEN
Biography

Born: December 16, 1775

Place of birth: Steventon, Hampshire, England

Mother: Cassandra Leigh Austen

Father: Reverend George Austen

Famous for: Writing some of the most popular novels in English, many of which have been made into movies.

How she changed the world:
Austen's social observations and understanding of women's place in the world and how families get along remain as accurate today as when she wrote her books more than 200 years ago.

Jane Austen said that if you GIVE a girl an EDUCATION and introduce her PROPERLY to the world, she will be able to SUPPORT herself and be fully INDEPENDENT.

Jane Austen

A QUIET LIFE

Jane Austen's father, George Austen, was a rector in the tiny village of Steventon in the English countryside 50 miles (80 km) west of London. By the time Jane was born in 1775, her parents already had five sons and a daughter, Cassandra. The family lived together in a rectory. With such a large family, it was hard for George Austen to support them all. He taught boys privately. The students lived with the Austen family in the rectory.

... it was hard for George Austen to support them all.

For the first three years of her life, Jane was sent to live with a foster family. This was typical among families of Jane's social class. This was the longest period Jane would be apart from her family for the rest of her life. When Jane returned home, she found the rectory constantly full of people. The nearest town was some distance away, so Jane spent most of her time in the company of her family, whom she loved.

In 1779, a wealthy relative named Thomas Knight stayed with the Austens. He and his wife did not have any children, and they grew very fond of Jane's older brother, Edward, who was then 12 years old. They later asked to adopt him officially. Edward became Knight's heir, meaning he would inherit his money and property.

Words that changed the world

In Pride and Prejudice, *Elizabeth Bennet writes about her first meeting with Mr. Darcy: "You shall hear then—but prepare yourself for something very dreadful. The first time of my ever seeing him … was at a ball—and at this ball, what do you think he did? He danced only four dances! I am sorry to pain you—but so it was. He danced only four dances, though gentlemen were scarce; and, to my certain knowledge, more than one young lady was sitting down in want of a partner."*

George Austen was the rector at the Church of Saint Nicholas in Steventon from 1765 to 1801.

Exploring the text

In this excerpt, Elizabeth Bennet is writing a letter about meeting Mr. Darcy. The story of their friendship is the basis of the novel *Pride and Prejudice*. She complains that he did not dance enough at a ball, or formal dance. This was considered bad manners, because there were strict rules about balls. Men were expected to ask women to dance. If a woman turned down one request for a dance, she also had to turn down all other requests. Balls were an important way for men and women to meet, and a highlight of village life.

HISTORY'S STORY

Jane Austen wrote about what she knew, which was quiet village life. Jane spent her own time sewing, chatting, writing letters (and, secretly, her novels), and walking in the countryside. Her choice to write about home life was unusual. At the time, the most popular novels were adventure stories and romances. They were full of action and very melodramatic.

BECOMING A WRITER

When Jane Austen was growing up, girls from Jane's social background rarely went to school. They learned to read and write, but it was considered far more important for them to learn domestic skills. Running a household, sewing, playing music, and learning good manners were seen as essential in order to become a good wife.

Southampton has a trail dedicated to Jane Austen's time there—but she disliked the city.

Going to school

Unusually, when Jane was seven years old she briefly attended boarding school in Oxford because her older sister, Cassandra, was going. Soon after the girls arrived, however, the school moved to Southampton on the English coast. Jane hated Southampton. It was a busy port full of sailors, many of whom came home sick with typhoid fever. Both Jane and Cassandra caught typhoid and were very sick. The girls' parents only found out when their cousin, who was at the same school, wrote a letter telling her mother how sick the sisters were. After they recovered, Jane and Cassandra carried on their education with their father at home. He let them read anything in his library of almost 500 books. Jane read a lot of plays, poetry, and novels.

In 1785, the Austens decided to send the girls away to school again. This time, they went to the Abbey School in Reading with their cousin. Jane and Cassandra liked the school. They spent the mornings in classes and had the afternoons to do what they wanted. Their time at the Abbey School was short-lived, however. It was too expensive and the girls came home for good when Jane was just 11 years old.

Starting to write

Jane loved being back home with her family. She had time to walk and think, and she decided to start writing. In the early 1800s, writing fiction was not seen as a respectable occupation, especially for women. But Jane wanted to write down the stories she heard from people such as her glamorous cousin, Eliza, who was married to a French nobleman. Jane would write stories and read them out loud to her family. Her stories were funny and witty.

From the start, Jane's female characters were not like female characters in popular novels of the time. She described strong-minded young women who wanted to marry for love rather than for money. This was uncommon for the time. Women in England in the late 1700s had no power. They could not own property and they had no rights. They had to rely on the support of their husbands or, if they were unmarried, like Jane, on their fathers or brothers.

In the 1700s, writing letters was popular because it was the only way to communicate with people far away.

A LOW-KEY CAREER

In 1788, when Jane was 13 years old, she visited London with her family for the first time. Her trip to the capital inspired more stories, which she wrote down in three notebooks. She wrote stories, short plays, and a history of England. Cassandra was a talented artist. She illustrated Jane's work.

As their older brothers grew up and left home, Jane and Cassandra stayed home with their parents. When they became teenagers, they started to attend balls and dinner parties. Both girls were attractive and popular, so they received many invitations. Meanwhile, Jane was writing stories based on their different experiences. Writing was not seen as an acceptable way for a young lady to spend her time, so Jane wrote in secret. So that only her family knew what she was doing, she would hide her work under another piece of paper, so it looked as if she was writing a letter. Her stories were about the people she met and the relationships she observed. The more she wrote, the more her writing developed. She created a style that was understated and witty. It did not sound like any other writer.

A supportive father

Jane's father took her writing seriously. On her 19th birthday, he gave her a small writing desk, a pen, and a supply of paper. This was a very generous gift, because paper was very expensive. Two years later, when Jane completed her first novel, *First Impressions*, her father read it. He decided it was good enough to become a book, and sent it to a publisher in London. Jane's name was not on the manuscript.

The Royal Crescent was built at Bath in the 1770s. It was one of the city's most desirable streets in Austen's time.

All Jane's work would be published anonymously during her life and for years after she died because she was a woman—and women did not write novels!

The publisher rejected *First Impressions*. Although Jane was very disappointed, she was determined not to give up. By 1801, she had written three novels, none of which had been published. Her father had retired a year earlier and the family moved from Steventon to the busy city of Bath. In 1803, with the help of her brother Henry, Jane managed to sell the manuscript to her novel *Susan* to a London publisher named Richard Crosby for £10. She had finally sold a novel! (*Susan* was later renamed *Northanger Abbey*.)

HISTORY'S STORY

While Jane and Cassandra remained at home, their brothers went out into the world. Henry studied at Oxford University before joining the army, Francis was a sailor, James became a minister like his father, and Charles studied at the Royal Navy Academy. Edward married and moved to another part of the country. The remaining brother, George, was disabled and went to live with a foster family.

CHAPTER 2

George, Prince of Wales, was also known as the Prince Regent.

REGENCY ENGLAND
Life and Times

Regency Period: 1811–1820

Named for: The Prince Regent (later King George IV), who ruled in place of his father King George III, who was declared unfit to rule in 1811.

Part of: The Georgian Era (1714–1830)

***Pride and Prejudice* published:** 1813

Political situation: England was at war with France during the Napoleonic Wars (1803–1815).

Jane Austen was WRITING during a TIME of ENORMOUS POLITICAL CHANGE. However, DESPITE these political changes, in Britain SOCIAL ORDER remained UNCHALLENGED. Austen was UNIQUE for her TIME because she CHALLENGED many of the ABSURDITIES she observed in SOCIETY.

ENGLISH SOCIETY

In the mid-1800s, Britain's growing industry was celebrated at an exhibition in London.

The world into which Jane Austen was born was changing thanks to the effects of the Industrial Revolution and the revolutions in France and America. English society was still dominated by rank, however. At the very top was the king, followed by the lords and ladies who made up the aristocracy. Beneath them were the upper classes, who were made up of "gentlemen" such as Mr. Darcy in *Pride and Prejudice*. Families who made their money from work or trade were looked down upon.

The world into which Jane Austen was born was changing ...

Land and money belonged to the aristocracy and the rich, who passed it down through their families. Poor families, who made up the majority of the population, rarely owned any real estate. They worked for the rich. There was no social mixing between the different social classes.

Jane Austen pokes fun at the snobbish behavior many of her characters exhibit not by directly outlining their social positions but by describing their attitudes and reactions to other people. Her heroines, such as Lizzy Bennet, eventually learn to see beyond someone's social standing to the real person underneath.

Words that changed the world

In Persuasion, *Sir Walter says, "Westgate-buildings! ... and who is Miss Anne Elliot to be visiting in Westgate-buildings? —A Mrs. Smith. A widow, Mrs. Smith .... my word, Miss Anne Elliot, you have the most extraordinary taste! Everything that revolts other people, low company, paltry rooms, foul air, disgusting associations are inviting to you."*

Exploring the text

Sir Walter has discovered that Anne Elliot has been visiting a widow in an unfashionable area of the city of Bath. Visiting the poor and sick was considered one of the duties of young women of Jane Austen's class. Sir Walter himself stays in the more wealthy parts of Bath up on the hill, where he can look down on everyone else. Jane Austen uses his words to reveal his snobbish attitudes. The spa city of Bath was a fashionable destination for genteel society. Jane lived there between 1801 and 1806, but did not like the city.

Bath was a fashionable place to visit. Its mineral waters were said to be good for the health.

HISTORY'S STORY

The Prince Regent, later King George IV, was usually in debt and was a figure of fun. As heir to the throne, however, he ruled in place of his sick father. That put him at the very top of English society and made him a trendsetter. The word "regency" comes from his title, and there are many streets and buildings in England named "Regent" in his honor.

RURAL LIFE

England was still a rural country when Jane Austen lived. Most people, like the Austen family, lived and worked in the countryside. For Jane, daily life was based around her family's home in Hampshire, first in Steventon and later in Chawton. She moved to Chawton with her mother and sister in 1809 after her father had died in 1805. She much preferred living in the countryside to living in Bath.

Jane Austen spent the last eight years of her life in the village of Chawton.

When the weather was good, Jane went for long walks in the countryside. When the weather was wet, she and her characters were forced to stay inside.

Most roads and paths were not paved and soon turned to mud when it rained. Travel was not easy. Most people walked everywhere. The rich traveled on horseback or in horse-drawn carriages. Ladies were supposed to travel only in carriages, while gentlemen could travel on horseback. Since horses could not travel too far each day, longer journeys took several days and were difficult.

Life at home

Jane spent most of her days at home, where she busied herself playing the piano, sewing, reading, and, of course, writing. In between her daily chores, she shopped and made and received visits. Unlike today, the mail in eighteenth- and nineteenth-century England was very frequent. Jane could write a letter to a friend in the morning saying that she would visit in the early afternoon, knowing that the letter would be delivered long before her visit took place. For entertainment, there were parties and balls to attend.

Prince George built himself a palace at Brighton modeled on an Indian pavilion.

Going on vacation

In Regency England, people did not travel abroad for vacations. They stayed in England. Some went to spas, such as Bath, to drink or bathe in mineral waters, which contained chemicals that were said to be good for the health. The Prince Regent had a palace built in the popular seaside town of Brighton, and people flocked there to copy him. At one point, Jane was supposed to vacation in the Lake District, a scenic part of northern England more than 200 miles (320 km) from her home. When the visit had to be cut back to just three weeks, however, she decided that the journey was too long to make the trip in time, so she did not go.

With no electricity, people lived by candlelight. During the winter months, the days were very short, making social calls much more difficult to carry out. Days were spent at home unless there was a social engagement. During the summer, it was easier to travel around and socialize.

THE POSITION OF WOMEN

At the time Jane Austen was writing, most women had little or no independence. Most had no education and they did not have a career. Poor women worked in the fields or in other people's homes, but for middle-class and upper-class women, their future prospects depended on marrying well.

... most women had little or no independence.

Women were not allowed to own property, apart from rare cases when they inherited a home because no male heir could be found. Women also had none of their own possessions. Everything they had belonged to their father before they were married, or their husband afterward. Once Jane's father died, Jane, her mother, and her sister were forced to rely on Jane's brothers for a place to live.

Jane and her mother and sister shared the same home.

A new home

In Jane's case, this meant that she and her mother stayed with one brother or another until they found a permanent home at Chawton. Chawton belonged to her brother Edward, who had inherited it along with another property from the Knight family.

Edward's wife had died while she was giving birth to their 11th child. Following the tragedy, Jane stepped in to look after the other children. To thank her, Edward allowed his sisters and mother to choose either of his properties, because he already had a home.

Tom Lefroy, who was romantically linked with Jane, later became the most important judge in Ireland.

For Mrs. Austen and her two daughters, having a home gave them independence and freedom. They no longer had to rely on male relatives in order to have a roof over their heads. By the time Jane moved to Chawton, she was 33 years old and had accepted that she would remain single. Having a house meant that she did not have to marry someone she did not like simply to make sure she had somewhere to live.

HISTORY'S STORY

Although Jane was single, she had had a number of romances, including one with Tom Lefroy, who later became the Lord Chief Justice of Ireland, and another with a minister she met at the seaside. She accepted a proposal by Harris Bigg-Wither, but changed her mind the next day. Cassandra was Jane's constant companion. Cassandra's fiancé died in 1797 and she never married.

TIMELINE OF REGENCY ENGLAND

The Prince of Wales

1795 Jane starts to write *Elinor and Marianne*.

1796 Jane starts *First Impressions*.

1801 Jane moves with her family to Bath.

1801 The Act of Union creates the United Kingdom.

1802 Jane declines a marriage proposal.

1802 The Factory Act limits the hours children can work.

1803 The steam carriage is driven for the first time. It is the forerunner of the automobile.

1804 Napoleon Bonaparte is proclaimed emperor of France.

1809 Jane moves to Chawton with her mother and sister.

1811 *Sense and Sensibility* is published.

1811 King George III is declared unfit to rule. The Prince of Wales rules in his place as regent.

At his coronation, Napoleon became so impatient that he placed the crown on his own head.

1812 The United States declares war on Great Britain.

1813 *Pride and Prejudice* is published.

1814 *Mansfield Park* is published.

1814 The first British police force is created.

1815 *Emma* is published.

1815 The first paved road is built in England.

1815 Napoleon is defeated at the Battle of Waterloo by the British.

1817 Jane dies on July 18.

1818 *Persuasion* and *Northanger Abbey* are published.

1820 King George III dies. The Prince Regent becomes King George IV.

American forces land by boat to attack a British position in the War of 1812.

CHAPTER 3

This house was used for a TV adaptation of *Pride and Prejudice*.

PRIDE AND PREJUDICE
Masterwork

Key facts about *Pride and Prejudice*:

Title: *Pride and Prejudice*

Original title: *First Impressions*

Written: October 1796–August 1797

Sold to publisher: £100

Published: January 1813

Author: Anonymous

Copies printed on first run: Approximately 1,500

Pride and Prejudice SHINES a LIGHT on what it was LIKE to be a WOMAN in nineteenth-century SOCIETY. It shows us how OPPRESSED women were and how LITTLE CHOICE they had in what HAPPENED to them.

INSPIRATIONS

Unlike most authors of her time, Jane chose to write about the world she knew. As she moved from one household to another, she had many opportunities to observe different ways of living and behaving in English society.

Jane and her sister often visited the homes of some of the wealthiest local families.

Jane and Cassandra were popular and were often invited to balls in grand houses. They sometimes stayed on extended visits. Jane studied the people she met. Men and women were meant to behave according to certain rules. Jane tried to look beyond the rules to see what people were really like. Her social position meant she was able to mix with members of the aristocracy, who were the social elite. However, meeting her father's congregation also allowed her to meet more ordinary people. She was able to write about the behavior of a wide range of people in her novels.

Men and women were meant to behave according to certain rules.

Jane knew that most girls in her social position were at the mercy of men. Getting married was essential. It gave a woman not just money but also a position in society. Many women married for convenience and not for love, but Jane opposed the idea. She created heroines, such as Elizabeth Bennet, who want to marry for love, not money. In this, Jane was very modern. Women in Britain were not taken seriously by most men. They didn't even get the right to vote until 1918.

Words that changed the world

In the introduction to Pride and Prejudice*, Austen writes, "It is a truth universally acknowledged, that a single man in possession of a good fortune, must be in want of a wife. However little known the feelings or views of such a man may be on his first entering a neighborhood, this truth is so well fixed in the minds of the surrounding families, that he is considered as the rightful property of some one or other of their daughters."*

Exploring the text

The opening to *Pride and Prejudice* addresses the issue of marriage, and makes it clear that it has very little to do with the idea of love. The passage says everyone agrees that a single man is clearly looking for a wife, and that families want their daughters to get married, whatever the husband's character. The only concern is to find a man with money. Jane's words are ironic. We later discover that the "universal" truth is in fact held only by Mrs. Bennet. Even her husband and daughters disagree with her, because they have a more sophisticated view of the world.

The book contains many examples of poor communication between men and women.

HISTORY'S STORY

The original title of *Pride and Prejudice* was *First Impressions.* One of the themes of the novel is that first impressions can be misleading, and that a person can allow his or her personal prejudices to influence how they behave. Jane took the title *Pride and Prejudice* from a quote from *Cecilia,* a novel she had enjoyed by the popular writer Fanny Burney.

WRITING *PRIDE AND PREJUDICE*

Candles were an expensive item in Regency England.

Jane Austen wrote *First Impressions* between October 1796 and August 1797. By then, she had already written her first novel, *Elinor and Marianne*, which would later be renamed *Sense and Sensibility*. She spent years revising both novels before they were published anonymously in 1811 and 1813.

Family entertainment

Pride and Prejudice has many descriptions of places, but its main feature is its many conversations. This reflects the fact that the book was intended to be read out loud. Jane wrote to entertain her family. At a time before electric lights and TV, families gathered together to find ways to pass the long winter evenings. The Austen family lived on a budget, and so would limit the number of candles they lit during an evening. They would gather and listen while one of them read out the latest passage from Jane's books. They discussed what they read, and Jane went away and revised the passage.

Jane wrote whenever she could during the day after completing whatever chores she had, such as sewing. She also had social visits to make in the neighborhood. Women of Jane's social class were not supposed to waste their time writing fiction. Jane kept quiet about her writing in public.

She was fortunate that her father supported her. He bought her a writing desk, ink, and paper so she could write.

Getting into print

Jane's first two novels were published long after she had written them. It was hard to get a novel published. When she finished *First Impressions* in 1797, her father sent the manuscript to a publisher. Reverend Austen had read enough novels to know his daughter's work was good and he was prepared to pay to publish the work "at the author's risk." This meant he would have to pay for any financial losses. Even so, the publisher turned down his offer. Jane would not get a publisher to buy a manuscript until 1803.

A slow process

In the nineteenth century, novels took a long time to print. Letters made from metal had to be arranged in words and lines to make a page of text, then printed on a hand press. By 1800, these printing presses could still produce only up to 200 pages an hour, so creating multiple copies of a book was a slow business. It was also very expensive, so writers often had to pay publishers to print their books. In order to disguise her identity, when Jane did finally publish *Sense and Sensibility* in 1811, the author was listed only as "A Lady." There was no mention of Jane Austen.

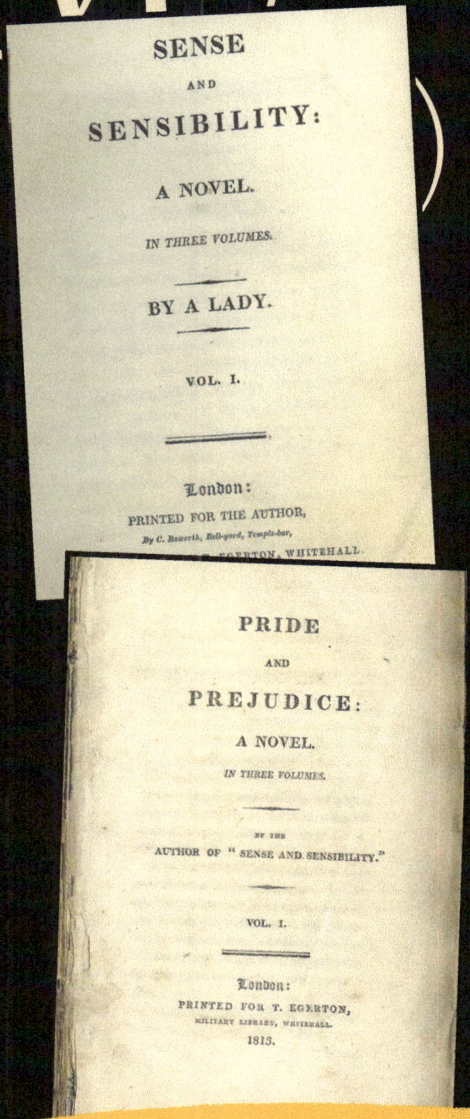

SENSE
AND
SENSIBILITY:
A NOVEL.
IN THREE VOLUMES.
BY A LADY.
VOL. I.
London:
PRINTED FOR THE AUTHOR,
By C. Roworth, Bell-yard, Temple-bar,

PRIDE
AND
PREJUDICE:
A NOVEL.
IN THREE VOLUMES.
BY THE
AUTHOR OF "SENSE AND SENSIBILITY."
VOL. I.
London:
PRINTED FOR T. EGERTON,
MILITARY LIBRARY, WHITEHALL.
1813.

When Jane Austen's first novels came out, it was rare for a woman's name to appear on a title page.

THE PLOT

Pride and Prejudice is the story of Elizabeth, or Lizzy, Bennet, the second of five daughters of a country gentleman, and her clashes with Mr. Darcy, a rich, aristocratic landowner. Although they like each other when they first meet, their respective pride and prejudice get in the way of them beginning to know and understand each other.

Elizabeth Bennet's mother, Mrs. Bennet, is determined to marry off her daughters. She is not concerned about them marrying for love. She wants them to marry for money. The girls' father, Mr. Bennet, wants his girls to be happy but he is aware that, as girls, they cannot inherit his wealth, which will eventually pass to a cousin, Mr. Collins. Mrs. Bennet hopes that Elizabeth will agree to marry Collins in order to keep the family home, but Elizabeth rejects the idea.

This modern poster illustrates various episodes from the story of the Bennet family and their friends.

In the novel, Darcy reveals his pride in his position and his prejudice against the lower social position of Elizabeth's family. At the same time, Elizabeth's pride in herself and her prejudice against Darcy mean that she does not see the real man. Eventually, they come to see each other's true characters, and they fall in love.

A constant theme throughout the book is how characters behave and how other characters judge them.

Other stories

The novel also tells the story of the friendship between Lizzy's older sister, Jane, and Darcy's friend, Mr. Bingley. Bingley's family has made its money through trade. Eventually, after various obstacles are removed, Jane and Bingley are also able to marry for love. The youngest Bennet sister, Lydia, is impetuous. She runs off with a soldier, Mr. Wickham, and causes a scandal. The two marry to save themselves from social embarrassment. Another marriage sees Elizabeth's great friend, Charlotte Lucas, agree to marry Mr. Collins, heir to the Bennet estate. When Charlotte marries for practical reasons rather than love, Elizabeth is shocked.

HISTORY'S STORY

At the end of the novel, Elizabeth Bennet's refusal to bow to convention and marry for security is rewarded. She guarantees her own social position by marrying a rich man, but she has also married for love. Jane Austen makes it clear that this is a marriage of equals, unlike the marriages of Lydia Bennet and Charlotte Lucas.

KEY CHARACTERS IN *PRIDE AND PREJUDICE*

Mr. Collins

Elizabeth Bennet	The heroine is the second of five daughters. She is quick to form opinions of other people. She is not motivated by money or social position.
Jane Bennet	The eldest Bennet sister is good-natured, pretty, and kind. She loves Mr. Bingley and marries him.
Mr. Darcy	A rich, handsome, and opinionated landowner, he falls in love with Elizabeth but is initially rejected before they try again and agree to marry.
Mr. Bingley	A wealthy friend of Mr. Darcy. Generous and easygoing, he falls in love with Jane.

Lydia Bennet

The youngest and silliest Bennet sister, she is obsessed with soldiers. She causes scandal when she runs off with Mr. Wickham.

George Wickham

He is a handsome soldier who wants to marry a rich woman.

Mr. Bennet

He is a country gentleman, long-suffering husband, and kind father.

Elizabeth Bennet and her father

Mrs. Bennet

She is an irritating and silly mother who is obsessed with marrying off her daughters.

Charlotte Lucas

Elizabeth's friend is practical and does not expect to marry for love.

Mr. Collins

A church minister and heir to the Bennet estate, he is obsessed with status and money.

CHAPTER 4

The Industrial Revolution changed the lives of everybody in Britain.

PRIDE AND PREJUDICE
Key Themes

Major themes Austen discusses in *Pride and Prejudice*:

The position of women

Courtship and marriage

Social class

Appearance versus reality

Prejudice

Pride

Outdated society

Money

Self-awareness

Austen COMMENTS on KEY ISSUES in nineteenth-century society, such as SOCIAL CLASS and MARRIAGE. She QUESTIONS what she considers to be OUTDATED beliefs, such as marrying for MONEY or SOCIAL POSITION.

COURTSHIP AND MARRIAGE

Mr. Bennet has not one but five daughters who need to be married to guarantee their futures. The laws of inheritance in Regency England were that only a man could inherit property. After Mr. Bennet's death, therefore, his family would be homeless. That makes the future of his daughters a great concern to Mr. Bennet, as their father. Girls of the Bennets' class could not work, so the only option they have is to make good marriages. Unlike many other fathers at the time, Mr. Bennet wants his daughters to be happy. Mrs. Bennet, on the other hand, just wants them to find good financial matches, but her husband understands that marriage is more than this.

... Mr. Bennet wants his daughters to be happy.

There was a complex system of courtship in the early 1800s to allow young men and women to meet one another. Strict rules of behavior had to be followed, and courtship was largely carried out in public on occasions such as balls and parties. A couple would never be allowed to spend time on their own, even if they met in someone's home. Courtships were also short. It was not unusual for a man to ask a woman to marry him after just a few weeks. Once a man proposed and was accepted, convention meant he also had to ask the woman's father for permission to marry. If the permission was given, the marriage took place, although fathers did stop what they saw as unsuitable matches. A woman was able to turn down a proposal, as Lizzy turns down Mr. Collins and, on the first occasion, Mr. Darcy.

Words that changed the world

In Pride and Prejudice, *Mr. Bennet tells Lizzy, "I know your disposition, Lizzy. I know that you could be neither happy nor respectable, unless you truly esteemed your husband; unless you looked up to him as a superior. Your lively talents would place you in the greatest danger in an unequal marriage. You could scarcely escape discredit and misery. My child, let me not have the grief of seeing you unable to respect your partner in life."*

Exploring the text

Mr. Bennet has learned from his own experience that marrying the wrong person will make life difficult. He does not want his daughter to make the same mistake. He is also aware that Elizabeth's personality—her "lively talents"—risks upsetting a husband who wants to control her. He warns Elizabeth that it is not enough to marry for love; he believes respect is just as important if the marriage is to be equal.

Strict rules decided who could ask whom to dance throughout much of history.

HISTORY'S STORY

Jane Austen knew from experience how hard life was for an unmarried woman. Unmarried women, or spinsters, were expected to help their married and elderly relatives. Life was hard because it was almost impossible to plan for a future when they relied on other people to support them.

WOMEN'S POSITION

Life for women in *Pride and Prejudice* is uncertain unless they are rich and independent, like Lady Catherine de Bourgh, or unless they marry well. Women in Jane Austen's lifetime had limited rights. They could not own property unless they had inherited it in a case where there were no male heirs. If they were married, everything belonged to their husbands, even if the woman had brought her own wealth to the marriage. If a woman was not married, her father owned everything.

Regency women like these two sisters practiced skills such as drawing and sewing.

Women of the upper social classes were not expected to be educated, and most did not go to school. Any formal education they received was often carried out at home with governesses and private tutors. Women could not go to college. Instead of being educated, women were expected to be "accomplished." This meant they needed to learn how to behave in smart society. They had to learn how to dance, to play a musical instrument, and talk in polite company.

The need for a husband

Marriage was the ultimate goal for most women. Elizabeth's friend, Charlotte Lucas, remains unmarried at the age of 27. This is considered old. At this age, she is prepared to marry Mr. Collins, whom she does not love, in order to secure a financially comfortable life. Once married, she plots how to get as much power as she can within the marriage without her pompous husband noticing. Elizabeth Bennet might not like Charlotte's decision, but she understands why she makes it.

This cartoon shows a man and woman playing music during their courtship.

Jane Austen is harsher in her portrayal of Lydia, the youngest Bennet sister. Lydia's silliness and obsession with men in uniform is her undoing. She thinks she is being grown up by running off with Mr. Wickham, but he has no intention of marrying her. Instead, he plans to marry an heiress who can pay off his debts. To avoid scandal, Lydia and Wickham are forced to marry. This condemns them to a miserable future.

A little freedom

Elizabeth and Jane are smarter than their sister. Having watched their parents, they understand that in order to live a fulfilled life they must marry men who are their emotional and intellectual equals. In these two women, Jane Austen shows her reader that it is worth waiting to get what you want and that it is possible for women to have a happy life by using the little bit of freedom they have—the freedom to say no to unsuitable suitors.

OUTDATED SOCIETY

One of the criticisms sometimes directed at Jane Austen and her novels is that they are not concerned with important events in Britain. For example, Britain was at war with France for most of Austen's adult life. The only reference to the war in her novels is the frequent presence of soldiers and sailors in uniform, such as George Wickham.

In fact, Jane Austen was very conscious that she lived in a world that was starting to change. Her use of irony in the ways she describes women in *Pride and Prejudice* suggests that she recognizes that they now have a chance to make changes in society. By making her heroines independently minded, Austen shows the reader what can be achieved when people force change.

The long British conflict with France only appears in the background of the novel.

The art of suggestion

Rather than spell out her ideas, Austen allows her characters to condemn themselves through their actions and words. She shows the snobbery of Lady Catherine and Mr. Collins to be old-fashioned. When Mr. Collins fawns over Lady Catherine's house, it makes him look like a fool who values appearance over character. Lady Catherine represents a social class that is stuck in the past. Mr. Collins, despite being only a distant relative, will inherit Mr. Bennet's estate because he is a man. Jane Austen suggests this is wrong by making him annoying. She implies that the law of "entail," which disinherits women, is wrong and unfair.

Britain was being changed by factories such as huge mills that wove cotton into cloth.

A new economy

In the same way, Austen shows how society in England is no longer based on the ownership of land, as in the past. Darcy's wealth comes from a huge estate, but Bingley's wealth comes from the new factories in the north of England. The Industrial Revolution was steadily transforming the country from an agricultural economy to one based on manufacturing. The rise of industry allowed people to make fortunes that were not based on inherited estates, which belonged only to the upper classes. Bingley's pleasant personality suggests Austen welcomes the coming of a new society, based on talent and hard work rather than inheritance. Few of these views are spelled out for the reader. Jane Austen is too subtle to do this. Instead, she represents characters such as Lady Catherine, Mrs. Bennet, and Mr. Collins as being snobbish and unattractive. They are stuck in the past, while characters such as Elizabeth, Jane, Bingley, and eventually Darcy look to the future.

JANE AUSTEN'S THEMES AND HEROINES

Sense and Sensibility (1811)

(Originally titled *Elinor and Marianne.*) The novel's major themes include romance, marriage, reason, and sensitivity. The heroine, Elinor Dashwood, is forced to move with her sisters, Marianne and Margaret, and their mother to a small cottage belonging to a distant relative.

Mansfield Park (1814)

Major themes include money, social position, and marriage. The heroine, Fanny Price, comes from a poor family that sends her at age 10 to live with her wealthy aunt and uncle.

Emma (1815)

Main themes include romance, marriage, social position, and the position of women. Emma Woodhouse is spoiled and wealthy. She interferes disastrously in other people's lives until she learns to be more accepting.

Mary Crawford from *Mansfield Park*

Catherine Morland
from *Northanger Abbey*

Persuasion (1817)

Persuasion introduces themes of class, social mobility, romance for older women, and second chances. The heroine, Anne Elliot, and her family have fallen on hard times and must rent out their home to earn money. This brings Anne back in touch with a man to whom she was once engaged.

Northanger Abbey (1817)

The book mocks the craze for Gothic novels while dealing with themes of loyalty, love, and social acceptance. Catherine Morland is young and foolish, but slowly understands that she does not want social acceptance or money but simply happiness and love.

Emma Woodhouse from *Emma*

CHAPTER 5

This illustration shows some of the inventions of the Industrial Revolution, including the locomotive and steamboat.

CHANGING BRITAIN
Effecting Change

Changing Britain:

Industrialization begins with the opening of mills and factories.

Great Britain loses its American colonies in the American Revolution (1775–1783).

Great Britain dominates Europe after Napoleon is defeated in 1815.

The Times newspaper starts daily publication in 1788.

Slavery is made illegal across the British Empire in 1833.

Great Britain (England, Wales, and Scotland) joins with Ireland to create the United Kingdom in 1802.

Industrialization was changing BRITAIN rapidly during the 1800s. As cities FLOODED with people who moved there for WORK, SOCIETY began to CHANGE and ADAPT.

CHANGING FACE OF BRITAIN

The first locomotives pulled open carriages for passengers.

The England Jane Austen wrote about was disappearing quickly by the time her novels were published, starting in 1811. The Industrial Revolution was gathering pace. Growing cities such as Manchester, in the north of England, were home to thousands of mills and factories. Powered by steam, the factories made parts of northern England very rich, like the Bingleys in *Pride and Prejudice*.

The steam power that was used to drive machines was also being used to power locomotives. The age of the railroad had begun. Paved roads also made other forms of transportation quicker. They shortened travel times until it took just two days to travel from Edinburgh in Scotland to London by the 1830s. Fifty years earlier, the journey had taken two weeks. The appearance of a daily newspaper, *The Times*, in 1788 meant people got their news at the same time across the country. The countryside was no longer as remote as it had been. Now it could be reached faster and news traveled far more quickly.

The age of the railroad had begun.

The rise of a new type of wealth also changed Britain. A new class of people started businesses and earned their own money. In the past, social rank had depended on inherited wealth. The new society would be less formal and based on achievement.

Words that changed the world

In Emma, we learn that "Emma's very good opinion of Frank Churchill was a little shaken the following day, by hearing that he was gone off to London, merely to have his hair cut. A sudden freak seemed to have seized him at breakfast, and he had sent for a chaise and set off, intending to return to dinner, but with no more important view that appeared than having his hair cut. There was certainly no harm in his travelling sixteen miles twice over on such an errand; but there was an air of foppery and nonsense in it which she could not approve."

Protestors known as Chartists riot to support more political rights for workers, including the right to vote.

Exploring the text

In *Emma*, the heroine is a young woman who values her own sensible behavior. Her surprise that a young man would rush off to London just to get a haircut shows the clash of the new and old worlds. Emma belongs to a period when people did not take off on a whim or do things simply because they enjoyed them. Journeys were long and had to be planned. Frank, who was raised in London, has a more modern view of the world. For him, making such a trip is not a big deal.

HISTORY'S STORY

The rapid changes in the first half of the 1800s led to a great deal of social unrest. The British government passed legislation such as the Great Reform Act in 1832, which allowed more people to vote in parliamentary elections. Groups such as the Chartists did not think the act went far enough. They called for every working man to have a vote, a goal called universal suffrage.

SLOW PROGRESS FOR WOMEN

Jane Austen was determined to make her own money by writing. When her brother Henry sold her novel *Susan* to a London publisher for £10, Jane was thrilled. She decided to keep writing so that she might have some money of her own. She earned 10 times that amount for her next novels, but they were still published anonymously, as women of her social class could not be seen to write novels. However, by doing so Austen paved the way for a generation of women writers.

Later in the nineteenth century, some of the greatest books ever written were written by women about women who lived much as Jane had lived. These were women from the upper or middle classes. They were still largely confined to the home and domestic activities. Women who were working class had no chance to write. They worked in mills and factories to earn money to support their families.

Anne (left), Emily (center), and Charlotte Brontë were all novelists. They published their first works under men's names.

Charlotte Brontë

In 1847, Charlotte Brontë published *Jane Eyre*. Brontë's heroine describes a woman's position in society 30 years after Austen's death: "Women are supposed to be very calm generally: but women feel just as men feel; they need exercise for their faculties and a field for their efforts as much as their brothers do; they suffer from too rigid a restraint, too absolute a stagnation, precisely as men would suffer; and it is narrow-minded in their more privileged fellow-creatures to say that they ought to confine themselves to making puddings and knitting stockings, to playing on the piano and embroidering bags." The passage caused outrage. Some critics said Jane's pleas for more freedom for women was as outrageous as the Chartists' call for universal suffrage.

George Eliot's real name was Mary Ann Evans.

George Eliot

In 1871, George Eliot published *Middlemarch, A Story of a Provincial Life*. It told the story of wealthy Dorothea Brooke, who longs to change the world and marries a much older man, Mr. Casaubon. She hopes that Casaubon will treat her as his intellectual equal but soon realizes that he will not. After his death, she learns he has written his will to disinherit her if she ever marries her friend, Will Ladislaw. By the end of the novel, she puts her happiness first and does marry Ladislaw. Dorothea does not change the world, but she finds happiness despite her first husband.

These novels and many others showed just how little life had changed for women during the Victorian age. It would not be until the Married Women's Property Act of 1882 that women started to gain some equality with men in Great Britain.

THE CHANGING FACE OF READING

Jane Austen's novels are more popular today than ever. Her concentration on everyday life and the way people interact with each other created a type of literature now called "domestic realism." Thousands of writers have been influenced by Austen's descriptions of family life and the process of courtship and marriage. When Austen wrote her novels, however, her approach was completely different from the most popular novels of the time.

Robinson Crusoe told the story of a shipwrecked sailor on a desert island. It was based on a true story.

Popular types of novels in the early 1800s included the gushing, sentimental romantic novel, the gory Gothic novel, and tales of adventure. Two of the most popular adventure novels from the late 1700s were Daniel Defoe's *Robinson Crusoe* and Henry Fielding's *The History of Tom Jones, A Foundling*. They were easy-to-read page-turners, and marked a change from most books people had read previously, which were usually far more serious histories, religious books, and tales of ancient mythology.

Power of the emotions

Sentimental novels celebrated the emotions. Some of the most popular included Samuel Richardson's *Pamela, or Virtue Rewarded* (1740) and Laurence Sterne's *Tristram Shandy* (1759–1767). These books helped lead to the rise of the Romantic movement, which dominated the early 1800s. Romantic poets such as Lord Byron and William Blake protested what they saw as the harmful effects of the Industrial Revolution. They concentrated on an ideal world they imagined before industry appeared. They suggested that this world was real and natural, unlike the artificial modern world.

The horror craze

The craze for Gothic novels began with Horace Walpole's *The Castle of Otranto* (1764). Gothic stories included fainting heroines, spooky buildings with hidden passages, curses, and the supernatural. The Gothic set out to scare the reader and could not have been further away from Jane Austen's world. The best-known Gothic novels, which are still popular today, were both written after Austen's death. They were Mary Shelley's *Frankenstein* (1818), originally published anonymously, and Bram Stoker's *Dracula* (1897).

In *Frankenstein*, a scientist uses human body parts to build a creature.

HISTORY'S STORY

Some of the greatest women writers of all time, such as Virginia Woolf and Emily Brontë, have acknowledged the importance of Jane Austen's work. Without her, they would not have written the books they wrote. Jane put women at the center of her novels and made their happiness her most important subject.

FEMALE AUTHORS WRITING ABOUT WOMEN

Fanny (Frances) Burney (1752–1840)

Evelina, 1778 (published anonymously)
Cecilia; or, Memoirs of an Heiress, 1782
Camilla; or, A Picture of Youth, 1796

Mary Wollstonecraft (1759–1797)

A Vindication of the Rights of Woman, 1792

Elizabeth Gaskell (1810–1865)

Mary Barton, 1848 (published anonymously)
Ruth, 1853
Cranford, 1853
North and South, 1855
Wives and Daughters, 1865 (unfinished)

A scene from *Evelina*, a novel by Fanny Burney

Mary Wollstonecraft (center) was the mother of the horror writer Mary Shelley.

Charlotte Brontë (1816–1855)

Jane Eyre, 1847
Shirley, 1849
Villette, 1853
The Professor, 1857

Emily Brontë (1818–1848)

Wuthering Heights, 1847

George Eliot (1819–1880)

Adam Bede, 1859
The Mill on the Floss, 1860
Silas Marner, 1861
Middlemarch, 1871–1872

Mary Ann Evans said she wrote under the man's name George Eliot so her novels would be taken seriously.

CHAPTER 6

Austen is still a best-selling novelist.

AUSTEN'S LEGACY

Aftermath

***Pride and Prejudice* key facts:**

Published in 1813 "By the Author of *Sense and Sensibility*."

Copyright of *Pride and Prejudice* sold for £110, although Austen originally asked for £150.

More than 20 million copies of *Pride and Prejudice* have been sold.

The book has been translated into 40 languages.

In 2007, it was voted the number one book in a World Book Day Poll.

Austen's novels were out of print for 12 years after her death in 1817.

Emma had the largest print run (2,000 copies) during Jane's lifetime.

Austen's novels have had a LASTING LEGACY. They have ILLUSTRATED history in a very PERSONAL and MEANINGFUL way and BROUGHT TO LIFE the fascinating INTRICACIES of the nineteenth-century WORLD.

A GROWING REPUTATION

Jane Austen's life reached a turning point in 1813. She published *Pride and Prejudice* in January. It was so popular that it was reprinted later in the year. By July, *Sense and Sensibility* had also sold out. Still, however, the public did not know the identity of the author.

The Prince of Wales enjoyed Jane Austen's books, which helped her popularity.

... Sense and Sensibility *had sold out.*

Jane set to work on her third novel, *Mansfield Park*. Her publisher worried that it was more serious than her earlier books and insisted Jane pay the printing costs. However, *Mansfield Park* sold out when it appeared in 1814. Her next novel was *Emma*. Jane had discovered that the Prince of Wales was a fan of her work, so she dedicated the book to him. Published in December 1815, it was the last of her books to be published in her lifetime.

Thirteen years after Henry Austen sold the rights to *Susan*, it had still not been published. Henry bought the book back from the publisher —and then revealed who the author was. The publisher was shocked to learn he had missed the chance to publish the writer of the popular *Sense and Sensibility*, *Pride and Prejudice*, *Mansfield Park*, and *Emma*.

Words that changed the world

In Emma, *the heroine says, "'I thank you; but I assure you you are quite mistaken. Mr. Elton and I are very good friends, and nothing more;' and she walked on, amusing herself in the consideration of the blunders which often arise from a partial knowledge of circumstances, of the mistakes which people of high pretensions to judgment are for ever falling into; and not very well pleased with her brother for imagining her blind and ignorant, and in want of counsel."*

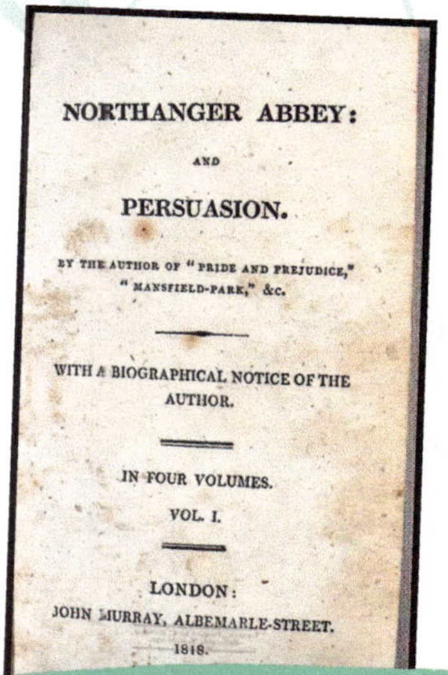
NORTHANGER ABBEY:

AND

PERSUASION.

BY THE AUTHOR OF "PRIDE AND PREJUDICE," "MANSFIELD-PARK," &c.

WITH A BIOGRAPHICAL NOTICE OF THE AUTHOR.

IN FOUR VOLUMES.

VOL. I.

LONDON:

JOHN MURRAY, ALBEMARLE-STREET.

1818.

Jane Austen's final novels were published in a single book after her death.

Exploring the text

Jane Austen's character Emma is one of the most flawed of all her heroines. Although she is wealthy enough to be independent, Emma is superior and judgmental. Over the course of the novel, however, she learns to understand herself better and also becomes humble enough to acknowledge her mistakes. She has failed to understand that her suitor, Mr. Elton, is only trying to marry her in order to secure her fortune. Jane shows how Emma overcomes her impatience with other people and how she learns from her mistakes to finally marry the man she loves, Mr. Knightley.

HISTORY'S STORY

Jane's last two novels, *Persuasion* and *Northanger Abbey*, were published after her death. *Northanger Abbey* was the new title of *Susan*, which she revised after her brother bought the copyright back from the publisher. Jane completed the manuscript of *Persuasion* shortly before her death in 1817.

A REVIVAL

By the spring of 1817, Jane was very unwell. Although she joked with her family about being ill, she was sick enough to write her will in April. She left most of her estate to her sister Cassandra. On July 18, 1817, Jane died at the age of just 41. She was buried in Winchester Cathedral in Hampshire.

On July 22, 1817, Jane's death was announced in the *Courier* newspaper. For the first time, the obituary revealed that she was the author of the four best-selling novels. To avoid people being critical of a female writer, however, the obituary also stressed that she was a lady, with good manners, and a good Christian. Even in death, Jane had to meet society's expectations of a lady belonging to her class.

More success

The Austen family was short on money, so they decided to sell Jane's two unpublished manuscripts. In December 1817, the publisher John Murray published *Persuasion* and *Northanger Abbey* in one edition. Murray paid £500, which was more than Jane had earned during her lifetime. With the exception of her first novel, *Sense and Sensibility*, publishers had bought the copyright of all Jane's novels. That meant Jane herself did not earn any more money, no matter how many copies the books sold.

Jane spent the last months of her life in this house in the town of Winchester.

In the joint edition of 1817, Henry Austen included a "Biographical Notice." He told readers his sister's story for the first time. For the next few decades, however, her reputation was not in the highest standing. In fact, at her funeral, the minister in charge of Winchester Cathedral wondered what she had done to earn the right to be buried in the old church.

This portrait of Jane Austen was included in the memoir published by her nephew, James Edward Austen-Leigh.

A famous fan

Jane's books were not republished for the 12 years following her death. A revival in her popularity started when the best-selling Scottish novelist Sir Walter Scott, author of *Ivanhoe*, praised her novels in 1826. Gradually, her work started to find a new audience. In 1869, Jane's nephew, James Edward Austen-Leigh, published *A Memoir of Jane Austen*. The memoir introduced all six of Jane's novels to a much bigger audience. More than 50 years after her death, Jane's novels were very popular once again. Since then, her popularity has grown and grown.

HISTORY'S STORY

Jane Austen's six novels were not enough for her readers. Over time, even her unfinished work has been published. She left 11 completed chapters of *Sanditon* when she died. Since then, many writers have "finished" the novel. Other unfinished works and Jane's childhood writings have also been published. All these works are still in print today.

JANE AUSTEN TODAY

Today, Jane Austen is more popular than ever. In the United States, she has a huge following of fans who call themselves "Janeites." There are hundreds of websites devoted to all things Austen, and Jane Austen festivals are held around the world.

The world Jane Austen portrayed has become a major tourist attraction. Her home at Chawton is now a museum. Walking around the rooms gives visitors a flavor of how Jane lived. The desk at which she wrote her novels is much smaller than you might imagine! With its original furniture and garden, the house is just as it was in Austen's day.

Bath, where Austen lived between 1801 and 1806, is the English city most associated with the writer today. It is possible to take a walking tour of the city to retrace her steps and to visit the locations she used for her final two novels, *Persuasion* and *Northanger Abbey*. The city is also home to the Jane Austen Centre.

A group of Janeites in Regency clothes parade through Bath during a festival.

Regency culture

During the Regency era, fashions were very distinctive. Women wore bonnets and long dresses in a French style called the Empire Style. Today, Janeites around the world dress up in the same fashions to enjoy traditional English customs such as taking afternoon tea. They might be less eager to experience many of the less comfortable parts of Regency life, such as traveling in carriages over unpaved roads.

Jane's home is now a museum preserved in the style of the Regency Period.

Lasting popularity

It is difficult to explain the growing popularity of Jane Austen's novels in the modern age. Her world was nothing like the modern world of social media and smartphones. Yet what she wrote about—love and families—remain exactly the same as they ever were. Look online and you will find hundreds of quotes from Jane Austen that are as true today as they were when she wrote them 200 years ago. Jane Austen understood human nature, and particularly women, better than anyone. She was also ahead of her time in calling for equality between men and women long before it became a common political cause.

HISTORY'S STORY

In 2013, the Bank of England announced that Jane Austen would be the first woman writer to appear on a British banknote, or paper money. The design for the £10 note was unveiled on the 200th anniversary of Jane's death on July 18, 2017. Alongside her portrait is the quotation "I declare after all there is no enjoyment like reading!"

ADAPTATIONS OF AUSTEN'S WORKS

Movies and TV adaptations:

Pride and Prejudice: 1940, 1980, 1995, 2005

Sense and Sensibility: 1971, 1981, 1995, 2008

Emma: 1972, 1996, 1996, 2009

Mansfield Park: 1983, 1999, 2007

Persuasion: 1971, 1995, 2007

Northanger Abbey: 1987, 2007

Lyme Park in Cheshire, England, was a setting for a TV adaptation of *Pride and Prejudice*.

Stoneleigh Abbey in Warwickshire, England, belonged to Austen's uncle, Thomas Leigh. Austen referred to it in *Mansfield Park*.

Loose Adaptations Based on Austen's Novels:

Pride and Prejudice:

Bridget Jones's Diary (1996) and movie of the same name
Bride and Prejudice (2004) Bollywood adaptation
Lost in Austen (2008)
The Lizzie Bennet Diaries (2012, YouTube)
Pride and Prejudice and Zombies (2016) and book of the same name

Sense and Sensibility:

From Prada to Nada (2011)
Scents and Sensibility (2011)

Lily James starred in *Pride and Prejudice and Zombies*.

GLOSSARY

adopt to make someone part of one's family
anonymously hiding one's identity
aristocracy the highest class in English society, based on property and family history
boarding school a school where students live
Bollywood the Indian film industry
bonnets hats that fold forward around the face
chaise a small horse-drawn carriage
class a system of organizing people according to their place in society, such as working class or middle class
colonies settlements in another country
copyright the right to sell a work of literature or art
counsel advice
courtship a period during which a couple get to know each other before becoming married
debts money owed
desirable describes something that people want
discredit a loss of respect
disposition a person's mind and character
domestic related to life at home
elite the people at the top of a society
estate a large property in the countryside
fiancé a man who is engaged to be married
fiction stories that are made up or imaginary
foppery behavior associated with foolish people
foster family a family that temporarily takes care of a child
genteel very polite and respectable
gory involving violence and bloodshed
Gothic a type of art or literature that is gloomy and horrific
governesses women hired to teach and look after children in their home
heir someone who will inherit a lot of money
identity someone's name and who they are
impetuous acting suddenly without thinking
independence the ability to make decisions for oneself
Industrial Revolution a period of rapid introduction of machines and steam power in the late 1700s and 1800s
industrialization the growth of industry such as factories, mills, and mines
influence to bring about change
inherit to receive property from someone when they die
ironic interesting or funny, usually because something is different from what is expected
locomotive a steam train
manufacturing making goods in a factory
manuscript a handwritten document
melodramatic exaggerated and highly emotional
memoirs books about people written by someone with a personal knowledge of them
mineral waters water containing salts and other chemicals
morality related to right and wrong
motivated driven to act for a particular reason
mythology ancient stories of gods
nobleman a member of the aristocracy
obituary an announcement of someone's death
occupation a skill used to earn a living
paltry of little or no value
pompous self-important
practical focused on doing things
prejudice a judgment or belief that is not based on reason or reality
pretensions ambitions to be superior
proposal a formal offer of marriage
prospects the likely success of one's future
rector a pastor who looks after several churches
regency a period when a regent is on the throne
regent someone who rules in place of a king or queen
respectable following accepted behavior
revival a return to popularity
rightful justified and natural
romances stories about love
rural related to the countryside
scenic with pleasant scenery
sentimental based on feelings rather than thought
snobbish proud and superior
sophisticated highly developed and educated
spa a resort with mineral waters
stagnation a failure to move forward
status how important someone is
suitors men trying to get women to marry them
supernatural unexplained and mysterious
typhoid fever a serious disease that causes rashes and stomach upsets
understated expressed without fuss or show
whim a sudden, light-hearted impulse
witty smart and amusing

FOR MORE INFORMATION

BOOKS

Austen, Jane. *Pride and Prejudice*. Edina, MN: Calico Chapter Books, 2011.

Fabiny, Sarah. *Who Was Jane Austen?* New York, NY: Penguin Workshop, 2017.

Sanderson, Caroline. *Jane Austen: Novelist*. New York, NY: Cavendish Square, 2017.

Santoni, Manuela. *Jane Austen: Her Heart Did Whisper*. Minneapolis, MN: Graphic Universe, 2018.

WEBSITES

Jane Austen Centre—www.janeausten.co.uk
Find out more about Jane Austen and the Jane Austen Centre in Bath, England.

Jane Austen in 41 Objects—
www.jane-austens-house-museum.org.uk/41-objects
This page tells the story of Jane's life in objects from her Chawton home.

Regency Period—www.janeausten.org/regency-period.asp
This page provides an overview of the Regency Period and how it influenced Jane Austen.

Publisher's note to educators and parents: Our editors have carefully reviewed these websites to ensure that they are suitable for students. Many websites change frequently, however, and we cannot guarantee that a site's future contents will continue to meet our high standards of quality and educational value. Be advised that students should be closely supervised whenever they access the Internet.

INDEX